Breaking The Word Curse

A Practical Guide to
Healing and Deliverance

Margaret G. Green

Copyright ©2019 Margaret G. Green. All rights reserved. No part of this book can be photocopied, stored, or shard with anyone except with the express permission of the author or as short quotes when properly referenced.

Scriptures (KJV) is taken from the New King James Version. Copyright © 1982 by Thomas Nelson. Used by permission. All rights reserved.

www.iamkingdomcreated.com

All rights reserved.

Paper back ISBN : **9781792746307**

CONTENTS

Forward

1	Introduction...	Pg. 2
2	Did You believe the Lie?........................	Pg. 8
3	How do you Identify yourself?..............	Pg. 11
4	Legal Access through Generational Curses.......	Pg. 14
5	Cursed Through Demonic Interference	Pg. 21
6	Cursed Through Witcraft........................	Pg. 33
7	Corrupt Communication Prepares a Grave.........	Pg. 36
8	Word Curses Through False Words................	Pg. 42
9	Hearing and Receiving Negativity..................	Pg. 46
10	Cursed through Emotions............................	Pg. 51
11	Guarded By Strongholds.............................	Pg. 55
12	Rejection's Deceptive Wall.........................	Pg. 58
13	Sleeping with Intimidation	Pg. 61
15	Fear Seals The Deal...................................	Pg. 64
16	Cursed through Rebellion...........................	Pg. 75
17	Breaking the Curse through Obedience...........	Pg. 81

17	Confessions to Breaking Curses.................	Pg. 85
18	Connect with Author Margaret Green	Pg. 110

Forward

Prophetess Margaret Green is an excellent example of overcoming the struggle of being cast down and being able to overcome trials that were inherited by the generation before her. This book will give you insight on how to recognize the word curses that have been released over your life and how to become free. Many people are delivered but not free, there is a big difference. Being delivered has to do with being removed from one place to another, being free has to do with your mind being renewed (retrained). This book will help you understand that your past or any word curse spoken over your life has no authority to hold you hostage and keep you from progressing. To get free from what's holding you captive, you must eliminate the emotion attached to the thought or words sent to defeat you and replace that emotion with gratitude because it worked for your good. If you remove and replace the feeling attached to that thought or word, you can get free from the curse.-
Prophet Jermaine Green

Introduction

Discovering your purpose can break any curse that has infiltrated your life. Where there is an identified purpose, there is also a standing promise from the Lord in which life also resides shielding against the grips of death. Word curses have the power to disrupt and block your God-given purpose from being fulfilled in the earth. You must start taking authority over the enemy and using the power through JESUS CHRIST to tear down words of destruction, strongholds, and closing open doors that give the enemy access to your life.

Matthew 16:19 I will give you the keys of the kingdom of heaven, and whatever you bind on earth shall be bound in heaven, and whatever you loose on earth shall be loosed in heaven

To bind and loose, you have to use your words. Words are so critical to a Christian's walk! We must be careful about the words we speak and the words we receive. When something tragic, unbearable, or life challenging happens, we assume we have been given a death sentence, and we automatically go into hiding. Not realizing that what we speak, hear, and how we receive can be very fatal and affect our Christian walk.

This authoritative life-changing guide will teach you how curses can form, how they manifest in your health, your mind, body, and everyday life. It will equip and give you simple keys to breaking word curses so that you may live freely in purpose according to the will of God for your life.

1 Peter 2:9 But you are a chosen people, a royal priesthood, a holy nation, God's special possession of him called you out of darkness into his wonderful light.

Curses will keep you in repeated cycles, blockages, cause sickness, bring lack, poverty, and little to no growth in your business, ministry, or church. It is always essential to discover the cause of curses. What is the reason the curse is being activated in your life and how to break it? Curses just don't come on you out of the blue. There is always a source, reason, or entity behind them.

Proverbs 26:2 As the bird by wandering, as the swallow by flying, so the curse causeless shall not come.

The most asked question is always why, Lord? Or why me, Lord? We still blame the Lord for why we are experiencing what we are going through, but we never stop to ask him the big What? What is the purpose of what I am going through, or what are you trying to tell me? Often the Lord may use sickness or a situation to bring you to a place of prayer and communication with him. Sometimes we are so busy with our lives, jobs, business, relationships, school, children, husband, or wife, and some of us are just busy with ourselves. You love the Lord, but somehow your relationship with him has been put on the back burner on low heat. Some of us are so consumed with negativity that we forgot about the one who gives purpose and makes it successful. Then there are times we fall into a state of giving up and allowing situations to helplessly take control over our lives.

No one is exempt from words curses operating in their life.. Often, it's the ones who pray for everyone else, the prayer warrior. You believe for everyone else, but indeed if you told the truth…there is doubt and a lack of belief for yourself based on the trials and testing you experience at times. But I want to encourage you today… The Lord is instructing you to speak those things that be not as though they were. Start believing for massive breakthroughs in your life because of God's will for your life.

Romans 4:17 *As it is written, I have made thee a father of many nations, 0 before him whom he believed, even God, who quickens the dead, and calleth those things which be not as though they were.*

There have been potent word curses of incompletion, not enough, lack, fear, inadequacy, and death that has been activated, opened or spoken, over your life that the Lord has given you power and authority through his word and the blood of Jesus Christ to break. When you are following and pursuing after God's will for your life, the enemy immediately launches an attack. Jezebel sent a message to Elijah telling him that since he had killed her prophets, now she was going to kill him. She told Elijah that she prayed that the gods will punish her even more severely if she did not kill him by the next day.
(1Kings 19: 1-3.)

Those were some pretty strong words to speak over someone's life. She spoke words of death that forced Elijah on the run. Elijah was afraid when he got her message, causing him to run to the town of Beersheba in Judah. As you can see hereafter Elijah receives the word curse, he leaves his help, and immediately walks through a dry place. After going to this place, he begged the Lord to just let him die. *(1 Kings 19: 4-5.)*

This does not appear to be the same Elijah that has killed all the false prophets of Baal. Before the words Jezebel spoke, Elijah was successfully leading the charge in displaying God's power. It wasn't until the word went forth from Jezebel about seeking to kill him that he did not stand on who God was and who the Lord had called him to be. He did not trust God's purpose for his life as a prophet to dismiss the word curse jezebel had spoken. What Elijah did instead, was ask God for the very word that Jezebel spoke over his life. He begins to ask for death. The curse had been so deeply rooted that it manifested on his lips. The word curse is on an assignment to cause fear, sow lies, cause you to receive death, to leave your help, to abort your God-given purpose, and to get you to believe and speak in favor of what the enemy is saying, while sending you into a dark, dry place of unproductivity called the cave with the result being total annihilation.

Often when the enemy speaks a word of death, we become frustrated, afraid, and angry, pushing our faith out the door. Truth be told that's when the real death sentence begins. We hide in a cave of sadness, despair, or grief; laying down our authority because we have allowed a word curse to activate in the heart of our faith. We replace faith with fear and purpose with death. But today, as you begin to renounce every word curse that has plagued your life, the Lord is undoing every snare and trap of the enemy. He is rewriting your story! He has already broke the back of sickness, diseases, and other things that may bring severe discomfort to your life through the sacrifice he made on Calvary, now its time to start walking in it.

1Peter 2:24 Who Himself bore our sins in His body on the cross, so that we might die to sin and live to righteousness; for by His wounds you were healed.

Did you believe the lie?

Curse-

A statement, word, or words used to deliberately bring harm, hurt, or to belittle. Words used to invoke a supernatural power to deliver damage or punishment to someone or an offensive or negative word or phrase used to express anger or a feeling toward someone.
Curse objective-
To kill, trick, deceive, blind, pervert, divide, hinder, isolate, limit, hold back, hold still, bring under, and cause death

Psalms 10:7 His mouth is full of curses and deceit and oppression, under his tongue is mischief and wickedness.

Did you believe what the enemy said about you? Did you believe what someone else said about you? Maybe you were rejected, and the rejection made you feel like you wanted to give up. You have told yourself…This is enough…I quit…I am done trying to figure this thing out, maybe the Lord meant for me to be alone, rejected, confused, sick, unprosperous, and isolated. Well, that is a lie!! That is not God's will for you to feel that way. The enemy will also try to isolate you from your help. Alone time away from the support means plenty of time for the enemy to work. The Lord did not create you to be alone, nor did he create you to be without an identity. Believing something about yourself that isn't true also opens the door for a word curse to take root and occupy space. The enemy talks to you as well, especially in a place of fasting and prayer. The enemy will make you feel like your ability, gift, and skill alone is the key. And if no one seemingly realizes that ability or gift that God has given you, you feel inadequate as if you are an automatic failure. This is farthest from the truth. The enemy took Jesus up into a high mountain and offered him all the kingdoms of the world only if he would bow down and serve him. Jesus already knew who he was and what his father had for him, which superseded what the enemy was trying to offer him. Jesus combated the enemy with the word of God. Can you tackle the enemy with the word of God when he puts your gifts before your face as bait for success? Allowing your gift, talent, skill to lead comes with a significant price. The enemy will always talk to your ability, not God's agenda, which leads to a curse.

John 10:10 The thief cometh not, but that he may steal, and kill, and destroy; I came that they may have life, and may have it abundantly.

Prayer:
Father in the name of Jesus Christ of Nazareth who is my Lord and Savior, the one and only King of Kings and Lord of Lords. I dismantle every lie, trick, and scheme that the enemy has sown in my heart. I pull up and pull out every seed and word of negativity

and discouragement that the enemy has lied and told me, that no one gets me, no one understands me, no one likes me, and things will always be like this. I am fearfully and wonderfully made as my creator has uniquely prepared me. My hands were made to prosper, and my feet were made for walking in purpose. I refuse and rebuke the voice of the enemy and every false word that he has spoken concerning my life in Jesus Christ of Nazareth Name.

How do you identify yourself?

We must be careful about what we call ourselves. Names are critical to who we are and if we are not careful, what you call yourself and what you allow others to call you could make or break you. The wrong name attached to your identity could be very detrimental to who you are. Words can curse or give life. Names house ability, responsibility, and or limitations according to your actions. Names demand a response; how you respond determines the outcome of your identity. We are all uniquely made down to our fingerprint design. No one is the same. We may have similar features, lookalikes, and even similar callings, giftings, and talents God has created us with, but we all possess a unique purpose that distinguishes us apart from the next.

You may often wonder what the Lord said concerning your life. Does God have my back, or did he just place me here without a purpose? Why am I always going through? Or why does it seem like this and that person is excelling, and I'm not?
Always remember that what you think about yourself is how you are going to perceive yourself. Negative thoughts breed adverse outcomes. If you feel like you are not good enough, you will always feel like you are not capable enough and strong enough to do what it is that the Lord has called you to do. Strongholds start in

your mind and manifest in our everyday activity. You are what you think.

It has been found true that when you change how you see a situation, it changes the whole scenario. How we review is how we use it. How do you view faith? How do you view belief? Is it something you feel like it's only for the moment, or is it something that only surfaces when things begin to happen and disrupt life? Ask yourself today…are you seeing straight? Is there something that has caused you to see with a skewed view? Or even see yourself in a negative light? What transpired? Did I say the wrong thing, did I do the wrong thing? Or maybe am I just super insecure with myself and feel like no one will ever accept me just the way I am? In order for anyone to accept you, or see you, you have to accept you. Love you, and everything that God has created about you. Sometimes It's not always the other person, it could possibly be an inside job.

1 Peter 5:8 Be sober-minded; be watchful. Your adversary, the devil, prowls around like a roaring lion, seeking someone to devour

Philippians 2:5 Let this mind be in you, which was also in Christ Jesus.

Proverbs 23:7 For as he thinketh in his heart, so is he:

Prayer:

Father, in the name of Jesus Christ of Nazareth, I take ownership of who you have called me to be. I am your daughter/your son and called with a great purpose. You created me in your image and knew me before I was formed in my mother's womb. My identity resides in you. I have been crucified with Christ, and I no longer live, but Christ lives in me. Because I receive you and believe in your name, you have given me the right to become your child. I rebuke and dismantle every single false word that has been released in the atmosphere, whispered in my sleep, spoken in secret, or directly to me by others and myself concerning my identity, my look, my name, my character, and my personality. From head to toe, I am blessed, and called according to the will, purpose, and plan of my Father in Heaven.

Legal Access Through Generational Curses

Often curses enter in through generational curses. We find ourselves seeing where we want to be and even getting so close to it, only not to obtain it. Our hopes and dreams quickly become shattered because we find ourselves following in the same pattern as our family members. If you take a close look at your family, you will see certain things that stick out that the majority of everyone suffers from. For example, you may notice that most of the women in your family suffer from bad relationships, abuse, divorce, loneliness, insecurity, anxiety, weakness, and health issues. While the men suffer from premature death, prone to accidents, not being able to get ahead, depression, alcoholism, drug abuse, suicide, and failed marriages. I remember feeling a substantial blockage. It was a barrier I could not visibly see, but I could feel it, and it was designed to keep me from receiving what the Lord had for me. I had prayed every prayer I could think of but still no resolve. I was binding and loosing, but yet nothing worked. It made me question and wonder. What door do I still have open that causes the enemy to have access to my mind? I started thinking about many different things but just could not come up with anything.

Praying and diligently asking and seeking the Lord for what was going on, I continued to pray. I felt the blockage and the stronghold in my mind. I went on a 21 day fast. The first day, nothing. The second day, it was hard. It was such a struggle to get in God's presence, it was like something was blocking my breakthrough. It wasn't until the 5th day in prayer I saw my great grandmother who had passed a few years ago. I did not fully understand the vision at first until the Lord made the vision more vivid and clear.

As a little girl, when we went to visit my great grandmother, she would pin dolls around her doorway leading into the rest of her home. I never understood why, only that she would become agitated if we took them down. There were even times we would stop by to visit and would see our dolls that we had left from the previous time pinned around the doorway. My great grandmother used to keep all types of games in her closet, but we were forbidden to go in her closet. However, I do remember walking in her room one night while everyone was in the kitchen eating and drinking and seeing her closet door open. Walking up on her closet, there were several Chinese games, chess, and a Ouija board. We had heard rumors that there were ghosts in the front parlor of the home leading into the dining area. The doorway with the dolls sat directly in front of that area. As I was praying, the Lord revealed my great grandmother and the doorway of dolls, which is an occult practice for warding off evil spirits. I was also reminded of when I was 13 years old and a few times as a teenager, my sister and I would call the psychic hotline to see if it was real or not. One time visiting the home of a soothsayer out of the desperate need for help, not realizing that I was turning God's face against me in anger, and opening the door for demonic activity and giving whatever curse that operated in my bloodline legal access to be released because I had committed idolatry. What I presumed to be fun and games at the time would soon cost me in my adult life.

Leviticus 19:31
"Do not turn to mediums or seek out spiritualist, for you will be defiled by them. I am the Lord your God.

Leviticus 20:6
"I will set my face against anyone who turns to mediums and spiritualists to prostitute themselves by following them, and I will cut them off from their people.

Ephesians 6:12 For we wrestle not against flesh and blood, but principalities, against powers, against wickedness in high places.

    I was instructed to repent and ask for forgiveness for the sins I committed and then repent on behalf of the sins of my great grandmother, and my ancestors who practiced witchcraft and instructed to renounce occult involvement and to renounce the spirit of witchcraft. I confessed Jesus Christ as my Lord and Savior and my redeemer. And declared that the curse was broken when he died on the cross. As I begin to repent and rebuke it, I saw a dark tower that sat on a hill caught on fire. The Lord revealed that there was a Wickedness in a high place at work through my bloodline but now through repentance and renouncing and obedience to his word, it was destroyed. By confessing our sins and wrongdoings, by the Grace of God, we can be forgiven and obtain salvation.

Exodus 20:5 Thou shalt not bow down thyself to them, nor serve them: for I the Lord thy God am a jealous God, visiting the iniquity of the fathers upon the children unto the third and fourth generation of them that share

Psalm 32:5 For I acknowledged my sin unto thee, and my iniquity has I not hid. I said I will confess my transgressions unto the Lord, and thou forgave the iniquity of my sin.

Romans 10:9-10
Christ redeemed us from the curse of the law by becoming a curse for us, for it is written: "Cursed is everyone who is hung on a tree.

Proverbs 16:20

Whoever heeds to instruction prospers, and blessed is the one who trusts in the Lord.

Ephesians 6:12
For we wrestle not against flesh and blood, but principalities, against powers, against the rulers of the darkness of this world, against spiritual wickedness in high places.

Open doors: Open doors will always give the enemy legal access to your identity. Often when things come to our mind, we try to rebuke and rebuke until we are blue in the face. We cast down vain imaginations, and those negative thoughts that come to our mind only to look up, and those thoughts are still present. The taunting did not leave. In desperation to see the word of God work in our life quoting scriptures but yet no resolve because the things we are dealing with are things that we allowed to enter through an open door.

***2 Corinthians 10:5** Casting down imaginations, and every high thing that exalted itself against the knowledge of God, and bringing into captivity every thought to the obedience of Christ.*

The problem isn't the scripture or decreeing and declaring the word in prayer. The question often is what is attracting those words or images to appear in your mind or those attacks. What access does the enemy have to you that causes even the words that you declare not to seemingly work? Are you still holding on to what someone has done to you in the past, are you harboring unforgiveness in your heart, entertaining conversations that you shouldn't, watching things that you should not, or involved in an unhealthy relationship? What open door is giving the enemy the right to attack your mind? You can't possibly declare the word of God over something that you are allowing and giving permission to be there. Every door must be closed to provide the word of God full access to dismantle and tear down every work and stronghold of the enemy that he sets up in your mind. God has His best in store for you. Only know that what you are going through is only a test. No matter what words have been spoken over you or what you may have thought about yourself, as of today, those words have been dismantled and broke off.

The storm may be rising, and the hard winds are blowing, but today JESUS has stepped on your boat. He has calmed the winds and waves of life and has now declared you whole. Today he has restored your faith to believe again in whatever situation you are going through, may be facing, or coming out of. He plans to get Major Glory out of your life.

Ephesians 4:27 Neither give place to the devil.

Deuteronomy 23:14 "Because the Lord your God walks amid your camp, to deliver you and to give up your enemies before you, therefore your camp must be holy, so that he may not see anything indecent among you and turn away from you.

Prayer:
Father in the name of Jesus Christ of Nazareth, Our Lord, and Savior, I repent and ask forgiveness for doing things I should not have done and allowing things in my life that should not be. I close every open door that has allowed the enemy to come and have access to my life, whether it was through my eye gate, my attitude, my thoughts, my ear gate, unholy choices, lying, association, relationship, fornication, disobedience, and sin. My life is not predicated on what my ancestors, my mother, my father, or the sins of my family. I am not a repeat of past failures, the cycle has been broken. You have given me a new life and because I am a new creature old things have passed away and all things have been made new. I am no longer bound by the sins of my generation or what those have done before me, neither am I a replica of their failures, downfalls, and disbeliefs. But I am a child of the Most High God. Walking in favor, success, and purpose! I will no longer be bound, hindered, blocked, unsuccessful, and without.

Curses through Demonic interference

Mark 9:17
And one of the multitudes answered and said, Master, I have brought unto thee my son, which hath a dumb spirit;

The deaf and dumb spirit affects how you hear and receive. This spirit attacks how you perceive words being spoken and how you release words from your mouth. It keeps you ignorant of the words you speak and of what you allow to come in and out of your spirit. This spirit also prevents you from hearing sound doctrine and applying the word of God to your life. Its total focus is to keep you without understanding and keep you in trials of fire with nothing to fight back with.

Mark 9: 18 And wheresoever he taketh him, he tore him: and he foamed, and gnashed with his teeth, and pined away; and spoke to thy disciples that they should cast him out;

Hosea 4:6 My people are destroyed for lack of knowledge: because thou has rejected knowledge, I will also reject thee, that thou shalt be no priest to me: seeing thou hast forgotten the law of thy God, I will also forget thy children.

This spirit will block a word curse from being broken because it keeps the cares, worries, and stresses of this world locked within while preventing the truth from coming in. Its purpose is to interrupt communication between you and the word of God for your life. The only way to know you are not oppressed by this spirit is when you can hear and receive the word of God, applying it to your life and seeing the manifestation. Don't be fooled, the enemy will also use your dreams and visions to communicate seeds of discord. He will sow seeds of sickness, untruths, and lies that are geared to release a curse. It is so vital that you are aware of the strategy of the enemy to defeat the word of the enemy.

Psalm 10:7 *His mouth is full of lies and threats; trouble and evil are under his tongue.*

I remember one time, falling off into a vision as I walked in the vision I was immediately approached by a demon. Its body was distorted and it hunched over. Its wrinkled skin was dark brown and it walked with a limp. The demon approached me and said you're going to die soon. Before I could react to what it just said, I snapped back and said: "Did GOD tell you that"? The demon replied, Oh a challenge, I love a challenge. The words the demon spoke would be the beginning of a significant challenging of my faith. The demon called Fear just challenged me according to the word and promise of God for my life.

After that, I did not give it too much attention or think about the vision much, although the words of the demon kept playing in my mind. I found myself going on a demon busting rollercoaster. Every day I was praying against sickness, I was rebuking death, I was pleading the blood of Jesus. Day in and day out. After many days and many months of doing this, I felt some peace so I kind of relaxed. I did not know what news I would soon receive.

Upstairs, I am cleaning my room one day, and our doorbell rings. It's a friend of my husband who is also a minister. He's getting ready to leave to move to another state. Although he was a minister, he was in the navy, and they had stationed him in another city. As they were saying their goodbyes, they decided to pray for one another. They were praying loudly. I could feel the power of the Holy Spirit from where I was in our bedroom. Until all of a sudden, my husband's friend yells out, " I rebuke the spirit of death, and the doctors made a mistake, I cover his wife right now in the name of Jesus.

It was almost as if time stopped…Wait a minute? What did he say? I hadn't been to the doctors yet. What is he saying? Admittedly I am a Prophet, and The Lord speaks to me, and he never said such a thing. Then all of a sudden, the words of that demon called fear begin to talk. See I told you were going to die. I began to rebuke its voice until it silenced.

That following Monday, I scheduled an appointment to take my physical. I was excited to get a clean bill of health. I felt confident because I had decreed scriptures over my health, and I stood firm in rebuking the voice of the enemy.
The scripture kept coming when Jesus was speaking to Peter about the plan of the enemy and his desire to sift him as wheat.

And the scripture in Job where the Lord offers his servant Job to be tested by enemy.

Job 1:8 *And the Lord said to Satan, "Have you considered my servant Job? For there is none like him in the earth, a perfect and an upright man, one that fears God, and eschews evil?*

I kept asking the Lord, what does this have to do with me? I didn't believe the Lord did not want to answer me, but I did not stay on my knees long enough for him to answer me. As the enemy's voice got louder, my prayers became shorter. What was going on? I thought. Was I losing hope? Or was it something much more?

I would continue to surrender my life, my gift, and everything to the Lord, not realizing I wasn't surrendering my mind and the words of fear that were trapped there. I could not understand how I was able to operate, lay hands on others and see them get liberated and free, but yet I was still so bound in my mind. I could not shake the fear of dying. My mind was in a total disruption. The Enemy started to build up a fort, and it all started through words.

It was finally time for my appointment. I prayed and felt great. I had just came from the gym. I lost a few pounds so I knew my doctor would be happy about that. I went in as my chipper self. How are you doing my doctor asks me? With a big smile, I said, I'm blessed. Any problems she asked. In my mind, I kept saying I need a test run on my colon, what if I have colon cancer. That does run in my family. Rebuking the thought, I looked at my doctor and said no, I am doing good. I did, however, remember an intermittent pain in my abdomen, but it was mild enough for me to keep it under wraps. The doctor looked at me again and asked, are you sure? Well, I do have a pain that comes and goes in my abdomen. But I don't think it's anything. Where is it she points? I point to the left lower part of the stomach. It may be appendicitis's I want to check to make sure it's not, but other than that you look good.

Green

They scheduled me for a cat scan down the hallway. After we finished the exam, I went and sat back down in the room where I saw the doctor. Me and my husband joking around and having a little fun. Thirty minutes later, the nurse comes into the room with a confused look on her face. Come with me, she said. She escorts my husband and I to my doctor's office where there is also another doctor, the head doctor over the practice.

Mrs. Green. We got your results back from your cat scan, and you don't have appendicitis. Just as I was getting ready to take a breath of relief, she says I am so sorry to inform you, but you have an abdominal dissecting aortic aneurysm. I chuckled and asked well what's that? The head doctor said, no this is serious we need to get you to a vascular surgeon right away.

You have a bulge and a tear in the major artery that supplies blood to your heart, brain, and lower extremities.

Everything slowed down. You got to be kidding me I thought. All that power and praying, and feeling the presence of Jesus and I still ended up with life-threatening illness? What was the Lord trying to reveal to me?

Right there, they scheduled the appointment to the vascular surgeon, and off I went. The vascular surgeon who was Asian was very kind and super young. I almost got discouraged based on how young he looked, only to find out he was much older than I was. Then the second call came. On the other end of the phone, the doctor speaks in a frantic tone, "Mrs. Green, we need you to get to the hospital immediately. You have multiple blood clots in both your lungs and one next to your heart." Now this took the cake. What a total shell shocker!

I started praying and fasting and asking the Lord to heal me. Most were moans and groans. I could barely make out the words sometimes. All I knew is that I could not stop talking because my life depended on it. Being reminded of

Psalms 91: 1-2

He that dwells in the secret place of the Most Highest shall abide under the shadow of the Almighty.
I will say of the Lord; He is my refuge and my fortress My God in him will I trust.

The enemy kept trying to speak, but I had words of life that now overpowered the words of the enemy. Praying through it, but seeing no results
Trying to pray and having your mind disrupt you with many different things. The thought of death and images of open caskets, demons, and sometimes pictures of illness. Afraid to go to bed because of the fear of a rupture happening in my sleep. Up at night googling people who had what I had been diagnosed with and finding that the survival rate was very small. I said Lord if I could only get my mind lined up with your word I will be okay. Always casting down many different things that would come to mind. Soon I begin to realize that not only the spirit of fear was present, but its brother intimidation was there, and he was alive. Right away with

the right opportunity to flourish and show himself, that's what he did. There was a door opened, but where? The only way the enemy could bombard me like this and get into my mindset to the point it starts to reflect on my everyday dealings in life. What door had I left open that gave the enemy legal access to my life?

Going back to the hospital, they wanted to administer a clot-buster, a medication that quickly dissolves blood clots but there was one problem. The dissected abdominal aortic aneurysm. They ended up sending me by ambulance to a Trauma 1 hospital where they were prepping me for surgery. After laying in the hospital bed awhile, the doctor walked in and said that they wouldn't be able to do surgery. They told me that if they repair the dissection aneurysm, the blood clots might travel if they remove the clots the aneurysm might rupture. They believed it was in my best interest if they did nothing at all. The doctors decided to administer the clot-buster but watched me to make sure that the aneurysm did not do anything. So if the aneurysm ruptures you only have a 5 percent chance of making it.

You can't be serious, at this time in my life I thought. The Lord had been speaking massive about purpose and ministry, but how could he talk to me about all of this when the doctors are only giving me a five percent chance of making it was the thoughts in my mind but on the other hand couldn't wait to pray to our Father in Heaven. This job was for him and him only.

The harder I prayed, the more the images became vivid. It was worse when I prayed inner because the sound of what I was seeing would often try to overpower the words I prayed within.
As I would pray louder, the images would disappear, and the sound of whatever was taunting my mind at that particular time would go. After fasting, praying, and seeking the Lord, he revealed that one of the doors the enemy was able to travel through was unforgiveness. I had left this door open without knowing it. I felt as long as I did not feel the pain and hurt from my past, I was okay. The Lord had revealed that I had numbed every issue in my heart

and locked it away. I had to forgive myself and those who had hurt me.

Instead of forgiving them, I did what I always did. I took out my little key, and unlocked the storage bin labeled hurt and pain and put it in there and it became numb just like all the rest. As long as I did not feel it, I felt like I was okay. I felt like I was ready for ministry.

The Lord revealed that I had hidden things in my heart; I told the Lord I was willing to forgive those who had hurt me in my past. As I began forgiving them, I felt the Lord doing spiritual surgery. Wow, I thought,

Forgiveness can be hard, but it is necessary. Often we feel like forgiveness is merely saying we are sorry or just moving past an issue, not realizing that the pain and hurt from the offense is still present and has only become numb within our hearts. True forgiveness says no matter what you did to me; it does not control my everyday life or my actions and love and trust towards others.

True forgiveness does not "feel a certain type of way" when the person is present or around. Often unforgiveness turns into bitterness and bitterness turns into numbness. For me, as I began to submit my life more to the Lord and move into the things he had called me to do, yes, this thing called purpose. He began to show me that I had held on to something that would not allow him to move any further in my life. Un-forgiveness is what the enemy was using as an entryway. He had been aware of the whole time that I lacked forgiveness. So the enemy was okay with me ministering, it didn't bother him much, because although I helped others get free, I was dying spiritually with a smile on my face, and for the kicker, I didn't even know it. For the bible says, (My people perish for lack of knowledge). It's essential to know the plot of the enemy and the word of God and how to use it and obey it concerning your life with a followed action.

Cursed through Witchcraft

Witchcraft

Witchcraft is the practice of seeking or practicing sorcery, magic, or wizardry. Witchcraft practices use familiar spirits, evil spirits, and demons. These practices are meant to curse, bound, chain, hinder, restrict, cause sickness, diseases, recurrent illnesses, and repeated cycles. Those who practice witchcraft speak words that are empowered by an evil supernatural force sent to release curses. They cannot release blessings. Some have sought out psychics, soothsayers, crystal balls, and hand readers who gave words concerning that person's life, some even being accurate words, but it was through the wrong source. The reading and words of psychics, soothsayers, horoscopes, and fortune-telling will bring about a curse because at that moment that horoscope or fortune-telling tool becomes your source instead of the Lord God Almighty. God is the only source and should always be our single source when we require direction for our lives. The bible tells us that witchcraft is an abomination in the sight of the Lord. The Holy bible lays out the consequences associated with Idolatry and worship to false gods. To rid yourself of curses through witchcraft, you must repent for all involvement, get rid of all cursed objects; candles, cards, shirts, charms, jewelry, crystals, healing rocks, peace rocks, sage burning, incense, and anything meant to influence your life and your environment. Witchcraft causes poverty, defeat, confusion, unexplained sickness, lack of finances, broken relationships, emotional dysfunction, division, and premature death.

The death of Jesus Christ breaks these curses. We must apply the word, his blood, and the authority to break these curses. We can be free of every curse pronounced by a witch or a warlock. We must first be delivered and redeemed from the curse of sin. We must be able to get the word of God to work on our behalf. Although the curse was broken when Jesus died, we must take responsibility and accept our actions; we must then repent, and then renounce the curse, and resist every attempt of the enemy to keep you in the curse.

Prayer: Lord Jesus Christ, I believe that you died and rose again on the cross. I receive you in my heart and life as my redeemer. Forgive me for all of my sins, past sins, rebellion, and all transgressions I've committed against you. I cancel and break every curse and renounce and rebuke any curse that has infiltrated my life through words, seance, gestures, chanting, objects, clothing, and words written. I confess the word of God over my life through the name, power, and authority of Jesus Christ of Nazareth, I am blessed, above and not beneath, I am the head and not the tail, I am blessed going in and coming out, Goodness and mercy shall follow me all the days of my life.

Corrupt Communication prepares a grave

Often we don't realize how much damage we do with words. Growing up as a little girl, not only being under the word curse of the name hard times, but my biological father released names that would eventually chain me to a dark place. Words of you're stupid, you're ugly, you don't look like me, you are clumsy, you're useless, often sent me into a dark place of depression. These words became so real; I believed every last one. Eventually, they started to manifest in my everyday life.

People often say that sticks and stones may break my bones, but words will never hurt me. This saying has to be one of the biggest lies ever told. Words have so much power to the point they can alter your life, manifest sickness, destroy friendships, change your identity, dismantle marriages, and destroy people's lives.

The words we speak about ourselves are not the only words we need to watch. What words have you uttered that has caused a cursed to be released over your life or maybe the lives of others? Perhaps you spoke a word concerning yourself of what you will never have and eventually ended up not having what you spoke in the atmosphere. Whether they were words of "I will never get married, there is no one out here for me, I will always be single, or there aren't any good men and women in the world, or I am not good enough. What words have you spoken concerning the lives of others? He or she will never make it, they are going to fall flat on their face, it will never work out for them, or they will never make it. Or even praying for God to do something to someone or praying for some mishap because you may or may not agree with a decision they have made. Speaking words of condemnation. You only speak what's within you. And with the same word curse, you pronounce over someone will also be the same words that come back to haunt you. Yes, we are also cursed by the words we speak concerning others.

Matthew 12:37

For by thy words thou shalt be justified, and by thy words, thou shalt be condemned.

Ephesians 4:29

Let no corrupt communication proceed out of your mouth, but that which is good to the use of edifying, that it may minister grace unto the hearers.

Sometimes with our children, they can make choices that may cause us to be upset. But we must be cautious at the words we speak over your children because what you speak is what you will see the fruit of. Those words of you're bad, you're stupid, you don't do anything right, you are just like your mother, or you're just like your father begins to manifest in their behavior and eventually in their life's decisions.

Matthew 12:36

But I say unto you; That every idle word that men shall speak, they shall give account therefore in the day of judgment.

Whether you thought what you were trying to accomplish, you could not achieve, or whether you felt like it was too hard, the words you spoke dictated the outcome. Or maybe you slide into the comparison game and feel like you could not measure up to those whom you esteemed, forgetting about the fantastic calling that was on your life. You stopped focusing on you and started focusing on them which provoked you to speak words of negativity concerning who God has created you to be. Sometimes it is merely receiving a word of condemnation from someone you look up to or someone you may admire and took their words as golden. Did they belittle you, or misread you because of your differences? You must also understand that people will also discount and speak negatively on things they do not understand. We often kill what we don't understand and disregard what we misunderstand. Often when people don't understand you, your calling, your gifting, or talent, they tend to want to discount, disengage, or kill it altogether. Sometimes it's more comfortable to disregard it than to pray and get an understanding. Often time this may be to lack of knowledge, not knowing how to use you to your strengths, traditions, what they've learned years past, or just done out of ignorance. More so often, this behavior isn't out of hate or a lack of love. They don't know, so they speak and operate according to their understanding.

Proverb 21:2

Every way of a man is right in his own eyes: but the Lord ponders the hearts.

Listen there will never be another you and no one can beat you being you, you will always be the greatest at being you, but a word curse can kill you especially if you are not sure what God is saying concerning you. People can say this or that, and may even assume things about you but the real truth of who you are residing with you and God.

Prayer:

Father, in the name of our Lord and Savior Jesus Christ of Nazareth I repent for all negative words I have spoken against, about, and to someone. I repent for all unrighteous conversations, ill will, gossiping's, strife, and unfruitful communications I may have had with others about someone else and myself. I rebuke the spirit of jealousy, envy, hatred, and insecurity that tries to attack and take over my life. I cancel every curse that has backfired, and that has entangled me through the words I've spoken about others and words I have spoken concerning my life.

Word Curses through False Words

Check the source of the information you are receiving. Where and who did it come from? Is it backed by the word of God? Do you know and are aware of the elements of the enemy's voice? The enemy's job is to speak words to you while you are spiritually weak that will divert you away from the truth. If you are not able to discern his voice over the voice of God, then you are susceptible to receiving a false word.

Word curses through false words or even trying to apply the right word at the wrong time or in the wrong season can bring on unnecessary captivity in your mind. Somehow when we receive a prophetic word, we never incorporate or seek the Lord concerning the timing of the word. We always want it now or automatically think that God is supposed to do it according to when we feel like we are ready to have it. Fortunately, everything works according to God's timing. The Good news is, if God said it, it would happen.

Both of these bring results that cause us to blame God when we don't see the manifestation of what was said. Receiving a promise too early can be very detrimental or receiving the wrong word for your life many false prophets will come to give you a word to discredit who God is. When a word is released without manifestation, it causes you to question God. God is not liable to back up something he didn't say.

That's why knowing God's voice is so important and what he is saying to you.

Jeremiah 23:16

Thus saith the Lord of hosts. Hearken not unto the words of the prophets that prophesy unto you: they make you vain: they speak a vision of their own heart, and not out of the mouth of the Lord.

1 John 4:1-2

Beloved, believe not every spirit, but try the spirits whether they are of God: because many false prophets are gone out into the world. Hereby know ye the Spirit of God: Every spirit that confessed Jesus Christ has come in the flesh is of God.

Deuteronomy 18 20-22

But the prophet, which shall presume to speak a word in my name, which I have not commanded him to speak, or that shall speak in the name of other gods; even that prophet shall die. And if thou say in thine heart, how shall we know the word which the Lord hath spoken? When a prophet speaks in the name of the Lord, if the thing follows not, nor come to pass, that is the thing which the Lord has not spoken, but the prophet hath spoken it presumptuously: thou shalt not be afraid of him.

Prayer:

Father, in the name of Jesus Christ of Nazareth, my redeemer, and my deliverer, I reject and uproot every false word that has been spoken over my life and into my life. I block, stop, veto, and cancel every effect and result of all false words spoken over my life by the power and authority of Jesus Christ!

Cursed by Hearing & Receiving

Discouraging words from others, adverse reports from doctors, failures, feelings, actions, and let downs can all contribute to a word curse forming over your life.

Often when we receive a diagnosis from the doctor, there is an immediate feeling or emotion that becomes attached to our spirit. The feeling or emotion, called "Fear." From that day forward if we allow it to incubate, it becomes intertwined in our mind, possessing our soul. The report may be accurate, but so is the word of God. What does he say concerning your body? Concerning your health?

I am reminded in Exodus 23: 25-26
And ye shall serve the Lord your God, and he shall bless thy bread, and thy water; and I will take sickness away from the midst of thee. There shall nothing cast their young, nor be barren, in thy land: the number of thy days I will fulfill.

By his stripes, we are healed and made whole. And with this promise, we are with clarity and consciousness able to declare healing in the name of JESUS CHRIST. Fear always lies about the outcome of a situation; it never tells you the truth.

The word of God, combined with faith, has the power to break curses that's been operating in your life. Jesus Christ spoke to the Canaan woman about her healing her daughter. When he spoke, her whole life shifted. First, she sought the one who could break the curse. Secondly, she confessed what the curse was and how it originated. Thirdly, she expressed her faith in Jesus's ability to perform it.

Matthew 15: 22, 27-28. And behold, a woman of Canaan came out of the same coasts, and cried unto him, saying, have mercy on me, O Lord, thou Son of David; my daughter is grievously vexed with a devil.

27. And she said, Truth, Lord: yet the dogs eat of the crumbs which fall from their masters' table.

28. Then Jesus answered and said unto her, O woman, great is thy faith: be it unto thee even as thou wilt. And her daughter was made whole from that very hour.

All she had to do was go back home, where the word of the Lord met her petition and see that it was done. One thing that Jesus did was that he did not ask her to bring the daughter to him. His word was already in route to her address as her faith went forward. You must believe that what the Lord has spoken, it is already in route to your situation, as a matter of fact, some of you his word has already worked a miracle. Although the mother was not physically there to see her daughter released the curse of possession by an evil spirit, she believed. You must believe that the curse is broken despite what you see or what you don't see? You wondered what you were doing wrong. And you gave up only to be stuck and unhappy because you are being fearful of stepping out on what the Lord has giving you to do. Listen the LORD

COMES and heals a thing or restores a situation in your life, at that very moment you have been reset and recharged.

Everything that is and was divinely supposed to happen in your life before it was interrupted with attacks, doubt, sickness, lack of energy, now can take place and happen.

The Canaanite woman interceded at the feet of Jesus in a place where there was no visible sign that the miracle or the healing had been performed but because she believed the word of GOD. She believed Jesus when he said he had answered her petition. That healing or the miracle had been performed was back at the home where she left it. Some of you have prayed and interceded for a miracle, but you never returned to see if I had done it. You can't pray defeated and expect a victory.

Today, I hear the Lord saying when you go back home, when you go back to the doctor's office, when you go back and get tested again, get another cat scan, MRI, blood work, can you believe the Lord for a change in the report. Even in your relationships, marriages, family, and friendships, can you believe the Lord for restoration?

The enemy can't reject what the Lord has accepted and protected. When you go back and approach that situation again, can you believe that all will have been restored and made new?

Prayer:

I rebuke every discouraging, belittling, demeaning, degrading, humiliating, curse from my past, negative words from leaders, supervisors, doctors, friends, family, past relationships, and those who I've come in contact with. I am not what they said I was. I don't respond but reject words of negativity. They have no power over me or my life. I am loosed and set free by the precious blood of Jesus Christ, of every negative word. I am blessed and full of God's favor! In the name of Jesus Christ of Nazareth.

Emotions and Actions that lead to curses

Jealousy

Noun-

The state or feeling of being jealous. envy, covetous; bitterness, spite

When we are absent of identity, purpose, and being under the pretense of a seed that the enemy has sown, we tend to despise the beauty, youth, success, talent, gifts, and skills of others. You tend to see them as a threat while seeing yourself as not good enough, old, ugly, unsuccessful, without identity, wanting validation, overweight, less than, not smart enough. Causing you to feel like God does not have a fair share for you. The parable of the servants with the talents in

Matthew 25:14-30 For the Kingdom of Heaven is as a man traveling into a far country, who called his servants and delivered unto them his goods. 15. And unto one, he gave five talents, to another

two, and another one; to every man according to his several abilities; and straightway took his journey.

Two things I want to highlight is that first, the Lord delivered unto to them his goods. HIS goods, not their own. So this means the Lord gives us all something unique and proper that he wants us to fulfill here on earth. No gift or talent has more value than the next. The second thing I want to highlight is that he gave them all according to their ability. The Lord knows what you can and cannot do. He knows what you can handle. The Lord, being just will never put more on you than you can bear. But we frequently look at what others are doing, and we compare, and we often try to take on or do things that weren't created to do. Do you have the stress level for that, the time and effort, the commitment, do you have the patience for it, how well do you deal with people? Can you suffer or pay the price they paid? These are some of the things we don't think about when we become jealous or when we are looking at what someone else is doing. And sadly while we are distracted looking at another, the GOOD thing that the Lord has given us to do goes buried.

Matthew 16 Then he that had received the five talents went and traded with same, and made them other five talents. 17 And likewise, he that had received two, he also gained other two. 18 But he that had received one went and dug in the earth, and hid his lord's money

Prayer:
Father in the name of Jesus Christ of Nazareth, my savior, my redeemer, who has liberated me and set me free by his precious blood, I will not allow my emotions to get the best of me. I will not receive what my feelings tell me because my feelings will lie to me. I rebuke every lie that my emotion has told me. I uproot every false word and negative word through my emotions that told me that I wasn't good enough, that I wasn't smart enough, that I couldn't achieve things in life, that said to me that I would never make it, that causes me to question who I am, and who

God has called me to be. Emotions that told me that people are against me, rejecting me, and not for me. I command every seed to be uprooted by the power and authority of the name of Jesus Christ of Nazareth! I will prosper, and everything that God has placed on the inside of me and given me to do will prosper double, triple, and quadruple!

Guarded by Strongholds

Strongholds

Noun-

A stronghold is a well-protected wall or thought pattern that does not allow you to be free.

It is an actual spiritual fortress built in your mind to guard against the truth. Most of those truths are of what the Lord is saying about you.

You often build strongholds, but the enemy maintains it. It is his job to make sure you don't get free, and he does that by feeding our minds with false and deadly thoughts often according to what you feel about yourself.

The good news is that the Lord gives us his word to combat stronghold and negative think patterns.

James 4:7 Submit yourself to God .resist the devil, and he will flee from you.'

Today the Lord wants you to surrender all of you to him. Submit your plans, submit your life, and put your total self on the altar. I don't care where you are reading this book, There is so much freedom for you, and the Lord wants you to experience every bit of it. Lift your hands and tell the Lord, "I surrender my mind to you today, Lord" I let go of everything that's in my mind that goes against your word for my life. Regulate my mind to think about the things you have set in place for my life. I renounce every stronghold that has been built by me. I rebuke every seed of discord, every seed that said I wouldn't make it, every seed that means I am not good enough, every seed that tells me I have to be someone other than who God has created me to formulated off the opinions of others. I am no longer captive by negative thoughts or recurring thoughts of negativity, harm, suicide, or death. I am made perfect in his image, and created with a great purpose In the name of Jesus Christ Our Lord and Savior, from this day forward I will not back away or avoid conflict with the enemy, but I will face him head-on with the word of God, for greater is he that is in me than he that is in the world. *(1 John 4:4)* I will not allow fear and intimidation to beat me up, I will not be afraid to be myself, but I will arise and be the courageous person God has called me to be. In the name of Jesus Christ, our Lord, and Savior.

Everything you are trying to handle on your own, He wants it all today. Let him take it over so you can ultimately live in freedom.

Rejection's deceptive Wall

Rejection

Noun-

The dismissing or refusing of a proposal, idea, to be rejected by someone or something

Rejection causes you to seek the affection of another or something. You try to pour your time and effort to that one thing that brings you satisfaction or that one thing that gives you the attention that you crave so much not realizing the enemy is setting up a strong barrier between you and the Lord (thou shall have no other Gods before me). The symptoms of rejection are feelings of being held back, not measuring up, being overlooked, undervalued, talked about, murmured about, not accepted, pushed down or pushed away, intentional dislike, Held up, no support, lack of support. The emotions of rejection are intermittent sadness, piles of anger, grief, wanting to go in a cave, hiding, trying to prove yourself. Rejection will also cause you to enter into a place of rebellion as well. Because we feel rejected, we make up in our minds to do something that will accept us, which is often the opposite of the will of God for our lives. We allow what we do contrary or that opposing act to what we are asked to do to be an excuse for the rejection that we feel. It causes our servitude to dwindle, we become unfaithful, and we start to take steps back.

The story of Cain and Able is a great example of how easy it is to feel rejected by God . He allowed his rejection to turn into anger toward his brother Abel. Which ultimately caused him to do the unspeakable. He killed his brother. Rejection will cause you to kill relationships around you. It destroys relationships, friendships, and if it's strong enough, even your marriage. Under the curse of rejection, you are not able to see people for who they are. Because you are under the control of that spirit, you don't realize that it's guiding your life and the decisions that you make. You say to yourself I like this person, but I am going to cut them off because of what they did. Rejection distorts your discernment and even causes you to resist help when it's necessary for fear of the way someone might look upon you, how they might perceive you, or misunderstand you. Opens the door to general curses and gives the enemy legal access to your mind and your thoughts. Rejection also has the judicial power to block you from discovering who you are in the earth realm. Your calling and your identity in God's Kingdom. It causes you to put in question everything that God tells you because you try to measure it according to the things you may have heard harmful or contrary to what the Lord has spoken concerning your life. You always seem to look for validation and when none is given you question what God has said thus allowing rejection to tell you who you are. Resentment manifests because you have now disconnected yourself and put up defense mechanisms. Your vision is skewed, and you watch everything they do with a fine-tooth comb, nothing slips by you. You watch and wait for little attacks here and small attacks there to further validate your reasoning

Sleeping with Intimidation

Intimidation

Noun-

The state of being intimated

    The intimidation assignment is to cause you to withdraw and to isolate. Intimidation brings unwanted pressure and heaviness. Often we become intimated when we feel insecure, less qualified, less anointed, less creative, less knowledgeable, and unaware of what to expect when situations arise or when we are facing opposition. Not being confident in who the Lord has created you to be will always cause you to become intimidated by other talents, other's success, gifts, and authority. You are easily discouraged by the challenge because you feel incapable. Intimidation quickly causes you to withdraw, backup, back out, and give up on your God-given assignments. It also causes you to fear the works of the enemy. Making you feel that you are not strong enough to fight off the works of Satan with the word of God. Intimidation will always cause a blockage in your mind keeping you standing still. Knowing who you are and being confident in the lane that God has called you to will defeat intimidation. Symptoms of intimidation consist of; when called upon there are excuses of why you can't do it, you suggest others instead of accepting a task given, you are passive, avoiding conflict, avoiding to speak up if you disagree, or feeling a reserve or the inability to voice your own opinion or how you think. Feeling the need to stay quiet in conversations that warrant your participation. Feeling inadequate around others that you presume are more educated, knowledgeable, and gifted, then you are. People who have fallen under the curse of intimidation are caught up by outward appearance, social media likes, and follows, and popularity, but fail to see behind closed doors. They become blinded by the outward success of another person making superficial comparisons to their own life.

David in the bible was not intimidated by his opponent Goliath, but those who surrounded him were intimidated based on the size of Goliath. Although they were all equipped with grand armor, swords, and shields to fight the giant, they allowed his size to keep them standing still. They withdrew themselves and refused to do what they were called to do, and that was to fight. They had allowed intimidation to keep them from using the weapons they had to win the battle. Because David was confident in the God he served, there was no giant tall enough, big enough, or too skilled that he could not face! Today, I prophesy over your life that you shall rise as David did, and you shall no longer be bound or defeated by the curse of intimidation, but you shall go forth with courage and strength because you are equipped to handle and confident enough to conquer and overcome any situation.

Isaiah 41:10 Fear not for I am with you; be not dismayed, for I am your God; I will strengthen you, I help you, I will uphold you with my righteous right hand.

Fear seals the deal

Fear

Noun-

To be afraid of someone or something

    The curse of fear will cause you to forfeit purpose. Fear of the unknown if it will work, if it will succeed, fear of rejection, making a mistake, people saying no, people not accepting and rejecting you. The fear of dying or not being successful or making it in life and fear of God's word not working in your life are all things we tend to allow us to go into a cave or resisting purpose. The enemy loves to incite fear into the children of God because it cripples the power and authority that God has given them to defeat him. Fear is debilitating. Fear sets up boundaries and repellents against people that are sent to help you and those who genuinely care for you. Fear also makes the word of God of non-effect. It comes to suck you dry of who you are. Fear will always use triggers of past failures, what people have done to you, and what you feel like you are lacking. The opposite of fear is faith. Which is a must to be used daily as your weapon to combat fear and anxiety? To rid yourself of doubt, you must decree and declare God's word with faith even if your faith is as small as a mustard seed. Faith to believe God that he loves you so much that he only has his good instore for you. But to have faith, you must hear and receive what the Lord is saying concerning your life.

2 Timothy 1:7 For God has not given us a spirit of fear, but of power and love and of a sound mind.

Deuteronomy 31:6 Be strong and courageous. Do not be afraid or terrified because of them, for the Lord your God goes with you: he will never leave you nor forsake you.

Romans 10:17

So then faith comes by hearing and hearing by the word of God.

Un-forgiveness opens the door to curses

Un-forgiveness often manifests into many different forms of distrust, skewed views, misunderstanding, false perception, and a lack of spiritual discernment, and even manifesting in our health. Unforgiveness is a silent killer. It has no respect for your title, position, authority, body, or life. It conquers whoever it embraces. Once unforgiveness takes root, it causes bitterness, anger, sickness, revenge, among other unholy thoughts or situations to occur, placing you in a dangerous position with God. We are going to be offended by what people say and the things they do, but we must forgive quickly because it gives the enemy legal access to wreak havoc in your life.

Colossians 3:13 Bear with each other and forgive one another if any of you has a grievance against someone. Forgive as the Lord forgave you.

Ephesians 4:26 Be ye angry, and sin not: let not the sun go down upon your wrath:

As for me, unforgiveness in my heart manifested in the form of a dissecting abdominal aortic aneurysm with several blood clots in both my lungs and one next to my heart. At first, I did not realize why all of a sudden out of the blue after being completely healthy, active in the church, and ready to conquer the world for Jesus that this would happen.

Although it may have looked like purpose and life had come to a complete stop, it was quite the opposite. The challenge to forgive ignited a divine push in me that would eventually catapult my faith, hope, and healing into another level. Instead of running away, I made a conscious and one of the hardest decisions to pursue forth with what the Lord had called me to do even if I had to die trying! I was had become so in love with doing the will of my father in heaven, that it didn't matter. "Faith and promise said to continue to preach, minister, and pray for others until you receive your healing. After hearing the Lord speak to me one day in prayer, he said I am going to use what was meant to kill you to heal you. Even though the doctors said death, The Lord used the sickness to heal my heart by causing me to forgive. He replaced all that numbness with his overwhelming love.

Romans 8:28 And we know that in all things God works for the good of those who love him, who have been called according to his purpose.

After forgiving and letting it all go, I went to the doctors. After performing tests, they came back and said all tests were negative. The dissecting aortic aneurysm had disappeared. There was no sign or trace of it. Because I had been diagnosed with a life-threatening illness prior, the images or words of "you're not healed" or "it's going to come back." I would find myself waking up and moving my legs around and twinkling my toes just to make sure the blood was flowing the way it was supposed to in fear of getting more blood clots and dying in my sleep. Some days afraid to go to bed because my heartbeat so fast from the anxiety of feeling like something was going to happen. Even though I had forgiven and received a total and complete healing, there was still something.

Ephesians 4:32 Be Kind to one another, tenderhearted, forgiving one another, as God in Christ forgave you.

Matthew 18:21-22 Then Peter came up and said to him, "Lord, how often will my brother sin against me, and I forgive him?

Forgiveness can be so very hard, especially when we have been hurt by those whom we love so very much. Whether it's church hurt, family, peer to peer, or relationship hurt the common denominator is hurt. Being misunderstood, and yes, that creates pain, being talked about, physically, sexually, or mentally abused; and seeing that person does something on the inside of you. Or maybe that situation tends to play repeatedly in your mind daily.

You are seeing that person advancing while you seem to be stuck on first base. You feel like you can never get ahead, all because of what this person, or what people have done to you. You may be asking what does this have to do with my healing?

Ephesians 4:31-32
Get rid of all bitterness, rage, and anger, brawling and slander, along with every form of malice. Thirty-two be kind and compassionate to one another, forgiving each other, just as in Christ God forgave you.

Our Father in heaven wants you to forgive to the point, when you see that person who has offended you, you are no longer getting that feeling in the pit of your stomach, or that one single nerve that that person used to strike is no longer reacting when they come around. But you are at ease, and you have released them according to what the word of God said. Peter asked Jesus how many times do I forgive? And Jesus, simply with love, replied seventy times seven. Boy, that's a lot of forgiveness, but you can do it. Put whatever the offense is on the altar and leave it in the Lord's hand. Yes, seeing that person does not remove what they did nor what they said, even if they felt like they were trying to help you. Or it may be out of his will. But unforgiveness binds you to that person, and you begin to take that person or those people into other relationships. You have to make a conscious decision that you won't allow people who have hurt you in the past to dictate to you your future. Which is one of the reasons why renewing your mind is so important? Our minds have been trained to believe whatever we allow coming in. We can either reject or receive what comes to our mind. That's why we must ask for a renewed mind daily. We must always be aware of seeds that are planted in our minds daily. The enemy knows if he can penetrate our minds with false words, past thoughts, thoughts of sickness, misunderstanding, offense, it tricks us into believing a lie while misguiding our perception ultimately creating prison bars that are locked and impenetrable called strongholds. All designed by you.

Romans 12:2

And be not conformed to this world: but be ye transformed by the renewing of your mind, that ye may prove what that good is, and acceptable, and perfect, will of God.

In a vision once; I awakened to an enormous serpent devouring my right hand. A sword came down and cut the snake in half. It fell off my arm, and my hand was restored as new. The Lord had revealed to me that night that the right hand represents authority, blessings, and strength. The sword symbolized the word of God, breaking the curse off my life. The hand being made new expressed whatever the enemy had taken, the Lord was restoring it.

Joel 2:25-26 And I will restore to you the years that the locust hath eaten, the cankerworm, and the caterpillar, and the palmerworm, my great army which I sent among you. 26. And ye shall eat in plenty, and be satisfied, and praise the name of the

Lord your God, that hath dealt wondrously with you: and my people shall never be ashamed.

The Lord said that everything that you tried to put your hand to have seemingly been devoured by the enemy. Your strength, your will to push forward. If the enemy can't get your vision, he will take your strength to do it. But I have cut off the head of the serpent, and he has fallen off your hand.

Joel 2:25-26 And I will restore to you the years that the locust hath eaten, the cankerworm, and the caterpillar, and the palmerworm, my great army which I sent among you. 26. And ye shall eat in plenty, and be satisfied, and praise the name of the Lord your God, that hath dealt wondrously with you: and my people shall never be ashamed.

You have experienced loss, defeat, and disparity. Some things have seemingly dissipated and come to nothingness. You were able to start it but never able to complete it, you always had an idea but no hands to help. Now you are going to experience the language of life what it means for a thing to flourish, what it means for a thing to be prosperous. What it means to experience wholeness in the mind-body and spirit!!!

Jeremiah 29:11

For I know the thoughts that I think toward you, saith the Lord, thoughts of peace, and not of evil, to give you an expected end.

Joel 2:28 And it shall come to pass afterward, that I will pour out my spirit upon all flesh; and your sons and your daughters shall prophesy, your old men shall dream dreams, your young men shall see visions.

Cursed Through Rebellion

Rebellion

Noun-

The action or process of resisting authority, control, or convention

1 Samuel 15:23 For rebellion is as the sin of witchcraft, and stubbornness is as iniquity and idolatry.

Because thou hast rejected the word of the Lord, he hath also rejected thee from being king. The truth of the matter is that no matter how much a word curse is prayed against disobedience keeps that curse intact. Failing to do the will of God and ignoring his warnings or his instructions. I realized that as long as I leaned to my understanding and did what I wanted to do instead of what God had willed for me to do, I would always remain under the rule of the name Hard times.

In the early years after becoming to know Christ, I had made a conscious decision sometimes to do as I wanted to do. I knew I had a call on my life, the prophetic anointing, or shall I say the gift to see was highly in operation. I had visions and dreams almost every day; I read the bible and could recite scriptures, but yet I refused to give all of me. In doing so, I did not realize how much rebellion I was operating in. I remember driving down the street on my way to do something I knew the Lord was not happy with, something contrary to his word or something that was against what he had spoken concerning my life In fear I would check to see if the sky was going to crack open. I would shake in awe on my way to sin. I was so afraid, but yet I was determined to follow through with what I wanted to do versus what the Lord willed for me to do. The tugging and the twisting and turning in my spirit wasn't enough to turn me around, but it was enough disobedience to cause that word to take root, rule, and take residence in my life. The more I rebelled, the more the curse took root. The voice of the Holy Spirit begins to become weaker and weaker while the spirit of fear and the word curse linked together becoming a strong force. One is affecting my natural state while the other affected by spiritual state.

Word curses will always affect your natural state. It is a word curse that will make you feel like you can't do this or that. Fear will continuously change your spiritual state. Fear is used to eradicate your hope and belief.

John 14:27
Peace I leave with you; my peace I give you. I do not give to you as the world gives. Do not let your hearts be troubled and do not be afraid.

Isaiah 43:1 "Don't Fear, for I have redeemed you; I have called you by name; you are mine."

It is your mind that tells your body what to do. It is your mind that tells you how you are going to go about your day. If your mind is under attack, it will not function properly.

The enemy doesn't stop at just taking your things from you naturally; he plays until he gets both. It is fear's number one cousin. And they love to hang together. But one thing about fear, since it's a dominating force and it tells intimidation what to do, once you get rid of fear, intimidation is automatically eliminated. It wasn't until I gave the Lord all of me and stopped rebelling against his word that the spirit of rebellion broke off me.
Going into a church service one night, I was to my wit's end. I no longer wanted to be bound. I was so fearful and afraid feeling like the Lord would not accept me back. I could feel myself fading away while something else took over. The rebellion turned into demonic possession. I recognized it, and I knew it was present. As much as I wanted to be free, I stayed bound. At the revival that night, I had twenty-five cents my sister had given me to put in the

offering. I was thinking, man, I can't put twenty-five cents in the offering. As I walked to put the money into the offering, the deliverance preacher Apostle John Francis stood at the altar. All of a sudden, I could feel my feet stop moving. No matter how much I wanted to proceed forward, something was stopping me. After a few minutes, the preacher came toward me. It was like he knew that something had ahold of me. As he came closer, the demon threw me to the floor. I started to scream uncontrollably. I felt like I was pinned to the floor. My body begins to form into a cross. My arms stretched from side to side, and my legs were straight. With authority, the preacher starts casting out every demonic spirit that was within me. He begins to cast out fear and also prophesy over my life, telling me about my childhood among many other things that I had suffered. I had started to feel my body jerk as tears streamed down my face. Green snot was coming out of my nose, and my shirt was drenched with sweat. I could feel the demonic presence lifting until it was gone.

Green

I felt free for the first time in years.

Breaking the Curse through Obedience

Obedience to the word of God will cut the hand of the enemy off your life. Disobedience will lead you to the curse. Sometimes we allow stubbornness and leaning to our understanding to cause us to disobey. You must stay in compliance with the word of God. There are no cheat sheets. Our flesh will always war against the spirit, but obedience is solely your choice. We cannot expect deliverance without compliance. We must follow the principles and the ways of living written out in the word of God. There are things the Lord is calling us to let go of, separate from, and stop doing, but because we enjoy what we do, God's word does not affect. God's desire is for you to live a full and joyful life, but disobedience can quickly cut that life in half.

John 14:23 Jesus answered and said unto him, If a man loves me, he will keep my words: and my Father will love him, and we will come unto him, and make our abode with him.

Deuteronomy 28:1-2 And it shall come to pass, if thou shalt hearken diligently unto the voice of the Lord thy God, to observe and to do all his commandments which I command thee this day, that the Lord, thy God, will set thee on high above all nations of the earth: 2 And all these blessings shall come on thee, and overtake thee, if thou shalt hearken unto the voice of the Lord thy God.

James 1:22 But be ye doers of the word, and not hearers only, deceiving your selves.

Deuteronomy 5:33 Ye shall walk in all the ways which the Lord your God hath commanded you, that ye may live, and that it may

be well with you, and that ye may prolong your days in the land which ye shall possess.

As hard as it may seem to submit and obey the word of God fully, you must do it to experience the true freedom that you seek. Checking in from time to time with God, or tiptoeing around what you're supposed to be doing will keep you in a stagnate place. You are wondering, crying, and feeling confused, questioning the Lord on why you are still in a tormented cycle. You constantly repeat the same trials over and over, year after year with no movement. Often, we are afraid of letting go of the control we have, out of fear of losing. Obedience gives God control and those who he has placed over our life permission to lead and guide us. When we become fearful of suffering, we resist compliance and ultimately live a life of disobedience. Whether we feel like we are being held back, the process is too long, others are going before us, or maybe you feel like you are not getting the same results as everyone, so you opt to do it all yourself, everything you do is about you, how you feel, and where you want to go instead of seeking the one who already laid out the blueprint for your life. As a result, everything falls to pieces, and you end back at square one because you now have allowed a curse called "repeated cycle" to enter in because of disobedience.

Confessions to breaking the word curse

Confession

Noun-

To reveal guilt, crime, or wrong, which is hidden.

To rid yourself of a word curse and any curse, you must confess the wrong and the error in your life and any crime you committed against the will of God for your life. Taking responsibility for your actions and not looking for any gray areas. We often do things in secret, whether it is using our mouth or tongue to gossip or speak ill will of our brother or sister, talk negatively, commit secret sins, or do things against the will and word of God. Things that you feel like no one will ever find out about. Not confessing your fault or offense will often cause sickness or torment. No matter what capacity you may be used in, if you are in offense, error, or sin, you are hindered from prospering and moving forward. We tend to offend each other, without ever taking ownership of the things we do, not realizing what we do and how we treat others renders the same effect on us.

Confession not only breaks curses off your life, but it allows you to be free from the burden of what you've done. Confessing your weakness and your areas of failures and not making excuses for them or blaming others for your actions. The enemy loves excuses. Excuses reinforce the word curse while securing the chains that hold you bound. You must also confess and release your faith in the Lord Jesus. Confessing your faith tells the enemy and every word that was spoken over your life that you believe the word of the Lord for your life and anything that does not line up has to go! After that, you must combine the word of God with your faith and obey and submit to the word God. Obedience and submission to the will of God will always release blessings, favor, and harvest over your life. Confess the sins that you are aware of and have knowledge of dealing with your ancestors. Forgive those who hurt, offended, transgressed, harmed, talked about, released negativity, abused verbally, physically, sexually, emotionally, and mentally. Lastly, relinquish and reject all involvement with occults, secret societies, associations, groups, and places or organizations that are against the word of God.

Prayer: Satan I decree and declare you have no more access to my life. Lord Jesus Christ, I believe that you are the son of God and the only way to God, that you died on the cross for my sins and rose again. I renounce all my sins and turn away from them. I receive truth and reject every lie and scheme, and trick of the enemy. I ask you Jesus for forgiveness, and I believe you have forgiven me I confess any known sins I have committed and the sins others related to me or my ancestors before me. I forgive every person who has ever hurt me, abused me, misunderstood me, misused, took advantage, rejected me, spoke falsely against, falsely accused, talked down, or belittled me. I renounce any occult involvement, and things that I have attached myself to that was ungodly and against the word of God.

1 John 1:9

If we confess our sins, he is faithful and to forgive our sins and to cleanse us from all unrighteousness.

Psalms 32:3-4

When I kept silent about my sin, my body wasted away. Through my groaning all day long. For day and night, your hand of displeasure was heavy upon me; my energy (strength) was drained away as with the burning heat of summer.

Letting go of past mistakes

Isaiah 43: 18-19 Forget the former things; do not dwell on the past. See, I am doing a new thing! Now it springs up; do you perceive it? I am making a way in the desert and streams in the wasteland."

The Past always seems to show up when we are facing some of the most stringent tests in our lives. Going back sometimes still feels like the best thing to do.
The enemy makes us feel like the Lord has forgotten about us that he removed himself from the equation. When he is the orchestrator of the equation, but the good news is he has set the problem up for a positive outcome. Past mistakes will also show up to show you where you are. The enemy's responsibility is to steal, kill, and destroy, and he can't possibly do that if he does not have you, so he tries to use his biggest weapon toward you. YOU. We are our biggest critiques, and sometimes we can be so hard on ourselves

that we give in to the lie that we are still the same person. The deception that the Lord never changed us and never did anything for us. This is only a trick to get you back into the same state you were in before the Lord redeemed you and called you free.
Yes, you are going to make mistakes, but you don't have to be the mistake you made. If God forgave you, then forgive yourself and move on.. You are way more victorious than what you think.

Philippians 3:13-14 Brethren, I count not myself to have apprehended: but this one thing I do, forgetting those things which are behind, and reaching forth unto those things which are before 14. I press toward the mark for the prize of the high calling of God in Christ Jesus

As much as you tried or wanted to break free, it seemed like you were in further and further. You couldn't pray even when you tried. Something feels like it is stopping you. You can't ask for help, and I know you aren't happy about that. It hurts because you feel and know you needed help. But this can only happen when you pull off the layers of the mask.

The mask often hides what we don't want others to see. Whether it's a smile, hiding behind works, makeup, or putting on a whole person other than who we are. You are pretending to be happy, pretending to have it all together. Only to realize what we are acting, and hiding is only fantasy. So the Lord allows trials to show up to reveal what's within us and who we are. Do you trust him the way we say we do? Are you a prayer warrior? Or do we run and hide in our tears when things seem to get super tight? Today is the day you pull off the masks and all coverups. Even the best concealer or face paint can no longer hide the anger and distress. It's time to wake up and free yourself of everything you have applied to your life that has consistently weighed you down.

It's time to stop going through life with a smile on your face, but frown in your spirit. Your head is down in the spirit, but because you are so used to empowering, encouraging others, and making sure their needs are met, you are so pumped for others but yet so empty for yourself. Take the time to allow the Lord to pour life back into you. His desire is for you to be filled with joy and have a productive life. It's time to smile again. The Lord is bringing the joy back

Romans 15:13 May the God of hope fill you with all joy and peace as you trust in him, so that you may overflow with hope by the power of the Holy Spirit.

Sickness, whether it's in the mind or body, will cause you to lay down. You can't afford to lay down when life is calling you to get up. This is not a time to lay in your bed with tears that have no healing power. This is a time to stand on the word of God with strong declaration and tenacity. Being bitter about life and everything around is not the answer. Bitterness is a sure way to kill whatever life is left. Through faith, hope, and belief, you can overcome the trials of life and those things that continue to push you into a place of sadness. You have to make a conscious choice to be the change you want to see in your life.

Isaiah 38:17 Behold, it was for my welfare that I had great bitterness; but in love, you have delivered my life from the pit of destruction, for you have cast all my sins behind your back.

We often speak words over our lives that the Lord has not spoken. Some may be for attention, while others, maybe because of the symptoms we may experience. But today I want to challenge you to stop self-diagnosing yourself and self-declaring life over yourself. Aches and pain will come, but you don't have to be subject to those pains. Your words have power, and whatever you begin to speak over yourself will eventually manifest, good or bad.

Proverbs 18:21, Death and life are in the power of the tongue: and they that love it shall eat the fruit thereof.

Because every curse that used to plague your life has been broken off, canceled, and dismantled, you have been given a new identity, and a new character calls for a new name. Now that every curse has been broken off of your life, you cannot be associated

with what you used to be or what you used to do in the past. Everything about your experience at this moment has been unlocked, unblocked, unleashed, and called forth into a place of promise, purpose, and prosperity! Often the enemy will use what we used to do or who we used to be to identify who we are. These are usually names and words of bondage geared to keep you afraid of purpose. Names and words that are opposite of who and how the Lord sees you. When you gave your life to the Lord, you no longer operated or for better words assigned to the name of what you used to be or do. You became a new creature in Christ Jesus. No doubt about it, the enemy will always bring up what you used to do, and sometimes even our minds can take us back depending on what situation we are facing. Jacob, one of Issacs's son's name, was changed to Israel, meaning May God Prevail. Before the name change, Jacob could not face what was in front of him.
Jacob was getting ready to face something significant. But he could not face it with the same name. Under the title, Jacob, was a

trickster, a liar, a deceiver. In the past, he had tricked his older brother Esau out of his birth rite.

And because he operated under the same name, he received in return what his name meant, who he was only attracted to what his name meant. Because he was a deceiver, he was deceived.

Genesis 29 And Jacob loved Rachel; and said, I will serve thee seven years for Rachael, thy younger daughter. And Laban said it is better that I give her to thee than that I should give her to another man: abide with me.

25 And it came to pass, that in the morning, behold it was Leah: and he said to Laban, What is this thou hast done unto me? Did not I serve thee for Rachael? Where for then hast thou beguiled me?

Now it came to the point where he was about to face his brother again. But he needed God's blessing to do so. He needed the blessing of a name change. With his new name meaning May God Prevail, said that now the Lord was leading his footsteps, he was in control, he guided him, and fought for him. The trickster had died, and now the Light of the Lord was visible. In my past, I had done many things, and the enemy never hesitated to remind me of those things. He made me feel incapable of God's love and God's "GOOD thing that he placed down inside of me because of my past. For years I buried my gifts and my talents all because of words. For years, I had operated beneath my calling and who the Lord had called me to be because of words. I had given up on life because of words. I walked in fear because of words. I allowed the enemy to make me feel inferior, weak, and unable to prosper due to the words of death that I allowed to resonate in my life. Words that did not apply to the Word that God had spoken concerning my life.

I want to encourage you today that your name has changed. You will no longer suffer hindrance because of words. Every word curse, negative word, word of death that was spoken over your life, your purpose, your calling, your talent has been canceled in the

Name of JESUS CHRIST. You are good enough; you are gifted enough, you are talented enough, you can build it, you can write it, you can design it, you can create it! Your body is whole and healed. Your hands are prosperous. You have power in the name of JESUS CHRIST to dismantle the attacks of the enemy, speak healing, and it comes to pass, decree, and declare, and it shall be so. The Lord has given you power and authority in the name of JESUS CHRIST to be free from the bondage of words and the chains they bring with them. Whatever talent the Lord has given you, it will succeed. It will prosper. Whether you have one, two, or Five, the Lord did not give limitations on how fast or how much growth it has. One talent can supersede the person with the five skills if you believe God and work with what he has given you. What you have is just as high as the next person. You are not what you did in your past, you are not what the enemy tries to whisper in your ear, but you are victorious in Christ Jesus. You are the head and not the tail. You are above and not beneath. I prophesy that every chain is broken, every stronghold is shattered with nothing remaining, every lie that has was spoken by the enemy or by others is uprooted now in the name of JESUS CHRIST. Insecurity goes, low self-esteem go, stress go, depression goes, lack of identity go, oppression go, heaviness goes, mind torment go. You shall live and not die. You are prosperous and shall have strength and authority. You shall no longer be misguided, stuck, halted, hindered, without direction or frozen in a state of limbo, in lack, but you shall and will proceed forward with direction and boldness in purpose! You shall use what God has given you, and it shall prosper 100, 200, 500 fold. Your work will not be in vain. You shall see a harvest. Your mind shall be filled with peace, joy, and your heart with love for yourself and those around you. You shall see different, and your eyes will not fail you. You shall conquer every devil, every obstacle, and attack that has launched against you. You are free, liberated, and released of every word curse that was spoken over your life! Now walk in it in the NAME OF OUR LORD AND SAVIOR JESUS CHRIST.

Notes:

Green

Notes:

Notes:

Notes:

Notes:

Green

Notes:

Notes:

Notes:

Notes:

Green

Notes:

Stay connected with

Prophetess Margaret Green

Facebook: @ProphetessMargaretGreen

Instagram: @prophetessmargaretgreen

Twitter: @MargaretGGreen

visit www.iamkingdomcreated.com

Prophetess Margaret G. Green a teacher, preacher, prophet, radio host, mentor, and author of *"Speak Into Your Own Life"* Now releases *"Breaking The Word Curse"*. A powerful guide that focuses on breaking curses off the mind through the power of decreeing and declaring the word of God and his ordained set purpose for your life. Discovering your purpose and the power that you possess on the inside has the ability to break any word curse that has infiltrated your life. Where there is a discovered purpose, there is also a standing promise from the Lord in which life also resides shielding against the grips of death. Word curses have the power to disrupt and block your God-given purpose from being fulfilled in the earth. It is imperative that you start taking authority over the enemy by using the power of authority through JESUS CHRIST to tear down words of destruction, strongholds, and close open doors that give the enemy access to your life.

Made in United States
Orlando, FL
24 November 2024

54363879R10071